YOUR SELF-ESTEEM GUIDE
TO A BETTER LIFE

RAULSTON B. NEMBHARD

Olde Wharf Publishers
8413 Clematis Lane
Orlando, Florida 32819

In conjunction with:
Old Mountain Press, Inc.
2542 S. Edgewater Dr.
Fayetteville, NC 28303

www.OldMountainPress.com

Copyright © 2011 Raulston B. Nembhard
Interior text design by Tom Davis
ISBN: 978-0-9713049-3-2

First Edition
Printed and bound in the United States of America by Morris Publishing
· www.morrispublishing.com · 800-650-7888
1 2 3 4 5 6 7 8 9 10

Contents

Dedicated to Dietrich on whose generation
depends the optimism and self-esteem
for a viable future

Acknowledgment

No book is ever the work of one person and so I am grateful to the many people I have worked with over the years who, in more ways than they would probably appreciate, have contributed to this small volume.

I am grateful to Lori Ginn who painstakingly did the editorial work for this book. Her meticulous grasp for details and her professionalism ensured that the book met the necessary standards of integrity. I am also grateful to Tom Davis and his staff at Old Mountain Press for their work in getting the book to print. Morris Publishing Company continues to do the printing world a great service. Their effort and expedition in this volume is highly appreciated.

My gratitude is extended to those of you who participated in the *vox populi* mentioned in the book. Your comments were valuable in placing my thoughts in perspective. Finally, my wife, Heather, has shown great patience in painstakingly reading the manuscript and correcting the proofs. Her valuable insights and suggestions have been quite helpful and kept me on an even course.

....
Raulston Nembhard
Orlando, Florida
November 2011

INTRODUCTION

Self-esteem, whether low or high, positive or negative, may be more important than many might have thought. The word is easily bandied around or glibly used in various contexts, but often people do not realize how significant it is to their success and purpose in life. I believe that this is especially so since the dawn of the recent economic crisis. Not only is self-esteem necessary for our own survival, whether rich or poor, but even for our mental, physical and spiritual health. This book is written with this truth in mind.

Self-esteem as I shall describe it here, is not a mere fancy or a passing feeling, but is in fact a state of being. It affects our lives in more fundamental ways than we may be aware of. It speaks to the beauty within us, the simple absence of which can lead to a distorted image of ourselves and our place in the world. These distortions are not merely situations which can or should be treated with medications (to which pernicious negative self-esteem may lead). Awareness of what drives these distortions will assist in the development of positive programs that can lead to meaningful and purposeful lives.

This book is not about a psychological or therapeutic approach to the subject. Many books have been written on the subject from those perspectives and there is no need to add yet another to our already crowded shelves. I am merely inviting the reader to a conversation developed over many years with people from all walks of life about a subject which many do not realize is not that well understood. My main intention is to help the reader to understand how important a healthy or positive self-esteem is for a successful and purposeful life and to have a clearer view of the things that lead to low self-esteem some of which might not have been seen as significant in the past. These observations will be supported as necessary with relevant anecdotes.

In this sense then, I am offering a guide on how we can achieve high self-esteem and avoid the many pitfalls that cause people to have a negative estimate of themselves. This is the main thrust of the book. If the book can help someone to a more holistic view of self or to take a new path that leads to greater fulfillment and meaning in his life, then I believe I would have achieved my purpose here. In the end, a high self-esteem is about inner beauty and how you can tap into it and stay tapped in securely. It is about finding and sustaining that inner beauty that lies within you.

There are powerful forces that fight against you attaining this inner beauty. Some of them are obvious to you, others are not. Some of them you have seen in your own life over the years but you have remained powerless to confront them. I will explore some of these forces in this book and expose the ones that might be less obvious. You will not always agree with what I have to say. The development of a high self-esteem is a personal matter and requires a personal battle which you have to fight and win. No one can do it better than you for no one can live in your skin, however thick or thin it is. My task here is to give you some tools as honestly as I can give them to help you in this battle of gaining and sustaining a high self-esteem. The rest is up to you. Let's begin the journey.

CHAPTER ONE

WHAT IS SELF-ESTEEM?

It is necessary at the outset to define what we are talking about, because self-esteem means different things to different people. If you ask a hundred people what self-esteem is you are likely to get a hundred different answers. Some might closely resemble each other or might be widely divergent from each other, for each answer comes out of a person's unique situation and circumstance.

I did a random sample of opinions, a *vox populi*, as to what self-esteem means. Here are some of the responses:

How one feels about self (this was the most abundant definition)
The views that shaped you from people around you.
Your thought or view of your own worth
A perception or sense of pride that one holds of themselves
How one sees oneself or what is my perception of who I am
How you view yourself; not necessarily how other people see you, but more about how you see yourself
How positively or negatively a person thinks about himself/herself

As you read these samples I can see you nodding your head most of the time for these are the standard definitions that are given by anyone when asked. I cannot tell you that you are right or wrong in your definition. This is not my task here.

Before explaining how I see self-esteem let me give you some standard definitions that have been given of the subject. The Oxford Dictionary, for example, defines it as "A favorable appreciation or opinion of oneself." Nathaniel Branden, a psychologist who has done a lot of work on the subject, says that it has to do with confidence in one's ability to think and to cope with the basic challenges of life and to have confidence in our right to be successful and happy (*The Six Pillars of Self-esteem*).

Most of the *vox populi* responses that I received stated that self-esteem is about how you feel about yourself at a particular time. To be sure, feelings are an important aspect of self-esteem, but as I will explain shortly, self-esteem is deeper than how we may feel at a given time. Feelings are too elusive and fragile to define what self-esteem is about. Most of the definitions that give feelings or mere emotional responses as definitions of self-esteem do not go far enough in really explaining what self-esteem is about. I believe that they do not give full service to the depth and breadth of the subject and may even undermine its importance in people finding the path to wholeness and fulfillment. It is true that low and high self-esteem will generate intense feelings or emotions but those feelings are the products of the state of self-esteem that the person has at a given time. To reinforce, self-esteem has greater longevity than mere feelings would suggest.

I do not believe you can give a neatly packaged defini-tion to self-esteem, so rather than trying to attempt that, I will describe it in these ways.

1. **Self-esteem is a state of being**. This places it beyond mere feelings and addresses the deeper sense of who we are-our sense of personhood, our identity (what has gone into our character building program to make us who we are) and our level of thinking about self. Seen in this way, self-esteem is not something that is fleeting or just a passing fancy, but is essentially a part of our mental, intellectual and spiritual makeup. I use the word "spiritual" not necessarily in the religious sense which is the way in which many people understand it, but to call attention to the deep yearning within every human being for meaning and purpose in his or her life.

As a state of being, there is a sense that self-esteem is pretty much a condition of the mind, heart and spirit. It is an abiding quality that suggests some permanence because it speaks to who we are as persons. There are persons who have been in almost a permanent state of low or negative self-esteem. Whatever has happened to them in their lives they find it difficult to feel elated about living. They may feel this way occasionally, but largely they have a poor estimate of who they are and how they fit into or fail to fit into good, holistic relationships. On the other side of the ledger, there are people who generally feel good about themselves and they live typically happy and fulfilled lives. There are different states of being to be in, and whatever level we find ourselves in is a true definition of the kind of self-esteem that we are enjoying. This is why self-esteem has to be more than just a mere feeling. Low or high self-esteem can generate any number of emotions, positive or negative, but these are just symptoms of the state of self-esteem that we have.

2. Self-esteem deals with the estimate, value or worth that we place on our lives. If we are living in a state of low or high self-esteem this will determine the value or worth that we make of who we are as persons. It is important to note that the word "esteem" comes from the same root as "estimate." To illustrate, if you have some plumbing work to do at your house you will call the plumber and ask him for an estimate of what the job will cost. What you are really asking him for is the value that he places on the job. This will be related to the cost of materials and the cost or value that he will place on his time and effort in doing the job. If you agree with the estimate, you give him the job and when he has performed it you pay what he asked for, if he followed through on his end of the contractual agreement.

This is hardly different from the value or the estimate or the esteem that each person places on his or her life. It might be farfetched to say that many people do not know what they are worth or how to determine what value they should place on their lives. Of course, I am not now talking about monetary value. To do so hearkens to an archaic mindset of human economy based on labor potential, such as indentured servitude or slavery. However, some people still live in a kind of slavery because they do not know how to actualize their true potentials. They live as bell hops waiting on other people to validate them or tell them what to do. The root word for "validate" is value. The point is, what value we place on our lives is critical to whatever state of self-esteem we find ourselves in.

High or low self-esteem does not arise in a vacuum. It is the product of important incidents or events in our lives that cause us to embark on certain detours on life's journey. Some of the reasons for these detours are pretty obvious, some not so striking. Part of my task in this book is to help persons to identify some of these drivers or events that prevent them from having a healthy estimate of their lives. Why is it that we often develop poor self-concepts that often leads to an indulgence in risky lifestyles, or cause our personal relationships to always go awry? Why is it that some children and even adults turn to bullying as a way of being accepted when their behavior is turning off other people? What about the parental culture in which we were brought up? Does this have a bearing on low or high self-esteem? It should be quite obvious that a state of low self-esteem will inevitably lead to suicidal tendencies because at some point the value of life becomes so consistently low that the best thing to do is to opt out of it entirely.

People who have a high value of their lives are not easily bowled over by criticisms. They do not spend their lives waiting on people to validate them or to allow other people's judgments to define who they are. They live comfortably in their own skins. But this is not easily achieved. It has to be worked on constantly. Our self-esteem may be impacted by external forces but how we choose to react to them lies deep within us. We should ask ourselves this question: Who am I and how much am I worth?

3. **Ultimately, self-esteem is about tapping into our inner beauty.** We are either internally beautiful because we have a high positive regard for self, or we are internally ugly for we have taken a very poor estimate of our lives. Our culture sells us the myth that beauty is an external thing and so the beauty industry has become a multi-billion dollar one today. Cosmetic surgeries have become fashionable as a result of this, as well. This is not to put down cosmetic surgeries or to stigmatize those who do them. There are very good and compelling reasons why these surgeries are performed. But the things that diminish the beauty within us cannot be removed by a surgeon's scalpel, for at the end of the day we will still have to deal with the hurts and the pains which diminish our self-worth and make us feel bad about ourselves.

The truth is that no amount of cosmetic surgery or beauty treatment can supply what inner beauty demands. While they can help us to feel good about ourselves and may even boost our self-esteem, there comes a point when we have to confront our inadequacies and the other negative things which prevent us from seeing the inner beauty that helps to define our intrinsic worth. It is never about the suit or the dress that the person wears but the person who is in that suit or dress. It is often not about the pretty face but the thoughts that circulate in the head behind that face. It is interesting that there are some people who are quite beautiful in their physical appearance who find it difficult to accept that this is so. This difficulty arises because they are not in harmony with their inner self. On the contrary, there are people who the world would not call physically beautiful, but who have come to accept themselves for who they are; they are strong and fulfilled on the inside and are able to accept themselves as being externally beautiful as well. They have achieved a harmony of external and internal beauty which is the greatest platform upon which to build high self-esteem.

To conclude: self-esteem is all about creating or finding value for our lives and coming to that state of contentment with what we have found and then living life to the fullest. No one can create that value for us; we have got to write our own estimate. Let me close with this story: A gentleman sat beside a lady on a flight from New York to Orlando. As they chatted for a while the gentleman suddenly said to her, "I will pay you $50,000 if you will sleep with me in my hotel room tonight." The woman appeared puzzled and mulled over the offer and then agreed. When the plane landed he said to her, "I have changed my mind. How about us agreeing for $10? She got irate, stood back, looked in his face and shouted angrily at him, "Who do you take me for?" The gentleman hardly flinched and said to her, "I have already established who you are; I am now just haggling about the price." The questions that each person must ask are:

Does my life have a price?

What value (estimate) do I place on my life?

CHAPTER TWO

HIGH AND LOW SELF-ESTEEM

We have seen that self-esteem can either be low (negative) or high (positive). Life, in a sense, is a rollercoaster of high and low esteem. Most people would agree that low self-esteem is characterized by a feeling of unimportance and unworthiness accompanied by a feeling of doubt concerning one's ability to achieve. High self-esteem is the opposite of all this as it is characterized by a high sense of pride in one's self-worth and great faith in one's ability to achieve.

From time to time people find themselves moving between high and low self-esteem. Either state does not have to be permanent. A person can experience low self-esteem because of a situation that he is going through (for example, loss of a job) and then experience high self-esteem as soon as the situation has passed. One does not need to be worried about this which I would call "situational self-esteem." In the course of a lifetime we are going to find ourselves moving between these two extremes. Real concern should arise if we find ourselves in a prolonged state of low self-esteem or worse what I would describe as chronic low self-esteem. The idea is to strive to achieve high self-esteem. This is not easily achieved. It is easier to slip into low-self-esteem than into high. When we move from high into low it is more difficult to get back into high.

One of the worrying features of the global economic crisis is that a lot of people have lost faith in themselves and even in life itself. Many who once felt proud that they could work hard and get a good education so that they can have a good paying job now find themselves on the dung-hill of unemployment. Many have lost their homes and many for the first time in their lives have had to turn to food banks and food pantries merely to have something to eat. Those who thought that they would never have to be on the government's dole and accept welfare handouts such as food stamps now join long lines to get the precious commodity. It is a matter of survival and people are resorting to any legal method to stay alive, hopefully until the storm passes.

In America, the harm that is being done to the self-esteem of the middle class is tragic. Some who have slid into poverty are now haunted by doubts as to whether the situation will ever be reversed. Those who have been unemployed for two years see no real prospect of staking their claim on the American Dream. The nightmarish existence in which they find themselves does not give any great hope of a future that is bright. Shattered self-esteem resulting in a loss of faith in one's intrinsic worth is never easily repaired. The longer the crisis of unemployment lasts the greater will be the level of unhappiness and the greater people's inability to restore pride, faith and trust in their ability to be worthy persons of society. Having a job is not just about collecting a paycheck at the end of a week or month. It is a spiritual exercise that gives meaning to who we are. John Allison, the longtime and now retired Chief Executive Officer of the BB&T Corporation, and a person who demonstrates high self-esteem, said in a recent C-Span broadcast that self-esteem is not given but earned by people who are better prepared to live their lives (*C-Span, 2008 Financial Crisis Causes and Consequences*, September 4, 2011). Essential to how we live our lives is a sense of pride in oneself and one's work. These are difficult to be regained once lost, he noted, as he bemoaned the persistent unemployment problem in the country.

Breadwinners, be they men or women or a combination of both, are particularly hard hit when they lose their jobs and their savings have dried up. They see their children going to bed hungry, they themselves going without proper healthcare and worry under the ever present threat of losing their homes. What these people need is not a handout from government or any form of welfare assistance. They want work, the ability to earn so that they can once again become highly effective, productive and capable members of society. People who live persistently in an environment of self-doubt will not be able to function at the true levels of their capabilities. They may come to believe that they are worthless and incompetent. Our policymakers do not seem to get this. Ultimately, it will not be about the trillions by which we reduce our deficit or how much we raise in new revenue and how much of our infrastructure we repair. It will be about lives that have been shattered, dreams that have been lost and the humanity that has been tarnished in people now having a low value of their own lives.

Parenting Culture and its influence on building self-esteem

There are many factors which impact our self esteem and one of these is the parental upbringing to which we have been exposed. It is not readily recognized how important parenting is to the development of self-esteem. I mention this here especially with the increasing cases of bullying in schools and the tragic consequences that this is having such as the increasing number of suicides among the young. We will come back to the topic of bullying later, for I believe it is essential to our discussion of self-esteem in the home. But, in very important ways, the kind of parents we have will directly influence the kind of person we become.

We do not get to choose our parents or the home in which we are born. In an important sense, the home is a controlled environment, a laboratory not just for socialization but for creating the essential person. There the parent or guardian will guard, guide and protect the young through the formative years of its life. Unlike other members of the animal kingdom, the human offspring has to depend on the parent not just for physical sustenance, but for moral and spiritual sustenance, especially through the first five years of that offspring's life, as child developmental specialists universally agree.

There are different kinds of parenting styles that are adopted in the rearing of children. I am not making any judgment about a particular style, for each style has its pros and cons. Most parents may not be preoccupied with any particular style in growing their children. I suspect that most just go ahead with the task at hand, not being aware or overly concerned that they are using one style or the other. So, the intention here is not to support a particular approach, but to help people to be aware of them and how they may impact a child in the development of low or high self-esteem. It does not hurt to know and at the end of the day the willing parent may want to take a look at his or her approach and may even come to the conclusion that there are adjustments that need to be made and behavior that needs to be revised.

The dictatorial or authoritarian style

This approach is marked by a rigid adherence to rules and regulations laid down by the parents. They do not entertain any challenge to these rules and any breaking of them is met with a strict code of discipline. Sometimes discipline is more informal but is often accompanied by violent language hurled at the child and in some instances physical abuse. Under this form of parenting, children are not encouraged to think independently or to have the freedom to express their thoughts about a subject.

Often under authoritarian parents children are driven by fear as they are cowed by the parents' bullying tactics. These children may go on to indulge risky lifestyles such as substance abuse. I have noticed in my dealing with adults who have suffered under autocratic parents, that in the case of boys, a demanding, autocratic father can have a marked impact on them. In an addiction facility in which I worked and where we had a number of group sessions with men, some would cry openly when they related how they were treated by their fathers. I recall one big, brawny, bearded man sobbing profusely as he related the horrors he endured as a child. At age 60, he could still recall with great clarity the days when his dad would drive up the driveway of his home. As soon as he heard the car he would run to his room and hide under his bed in fear that his dad was going to blame him for something he did not do. He knew that this would result in him being spanked or otherwise mistreated.

Some expressed with great remorse the thought that at no time did they ever hear the magic words from their dad's mouth, "Son, I love you." There were no hugs, no kisses, only blame and demeaning words hurled at them about how worthless they were and how they would not amount to anything much. Many were convinced that they turned to a life of drug abuse precisely because they were crippled in their minds by these self-defeating thoughts that were poured constantly into them. Very seldom would you hear of a mother abusing a child in this way, but in many a household the mother is sometimes careful to intervene from fear of being set upon herself.

It is hard to measure how self-affirming it is for a child to be told that he or she is loved or how powerful it is to feel the warm arms of a parent embracing a child especially when the child knows that he or she deserves to be hugged. How devastating for a child's self-esteem (reminder: value of self) to be cursed at, called demeaning names or otherwise berated by an uncaring parent who frankly has forfeited the right to be a parent. They have forfeited this right because every child has a right to be brought up in an environment in which they feel secure and protected, not one in which fear dominates.

If you have been exposed to this kind of parenting and you believe that your self-esteem has suffered as a result of it, all is not lost. I have known many children who have grown up under dictatorial or autocratic parents, who have gone on to live fulfilled and successful lives. They will tell you that the road upon which they have come was not easy. They had to struggle against great odds and they will admit that even now the struggle is not over, but they are pressing on knowing that they are made of sterner stuff than their parents made them out to have. If you are going through a big struggle with low self-esteem you may want to reflect on the kind of parents you had in your life. If your issue is one of independence or an inability to trust your own judgments, you may be able to make the connection between what you are going through now and whether your parents are still sitting in your life as the big elephant to be politely shown the exit. If you are a parent reading this and you know that you have run your household like a tyrant, there is work to be done. You may help your self-esteem by picking up the phone and making a call and start expressing some real regrets to those you claimed to love but never really did. This is hard to do, but for your sake and those you might have hurt, it is something that needs to be done.

Laissez-faire parenting
Laissez-faire is a French term which means "let do, let go, let pass." By laissez-faire I simply mean letting people do as they please. When related to parenting it is a style in which parents allow their children to do pretty much what they wish without the constraint of discipline or guidance. It goes to the other extreme of dictatorial parenting for there are no rules or mechanism established to regulate

behavior. There is little or no boundary established to keep children in check.

Research has shown that children raised in this kind of environment tend to be rebellious, disobedient and lacking in self-control as they grow older. They tend to perform poorly in school and exhibit deviant and otherwise disruptive behavior from an early age. Children need boundaries and it is the duty of responsible parents to establish these boundaries early in the children's lives. Boundaries should not be rigid, as Dr. Henry Cloud notes in his bestselling book, *Boundaries*, but they must provide the flexibility in which the child is encouraged to think and act freely without fear. Where there are no boundaries there can only be chaos. The child will roam freely and others can come and go at will exposing children to corrupting influences as there is a free for all.

Children sometimes cry out for these boundaries. The mistake that some parents make is to assume that they can be chummy with their children and expose them to adult thinking before they are old enough to be so exposed. A child as a "best friend" is something to be treated with great caution. There is a distinct role that the parent has and this cannot be eroded simply to be on friendly terms with the child. Many teenagers who rebel crave for boundaries, but in laissez-faire parenting, the parents have been so lax in providing these that many of them do not know what to do when the child begins to rebel. Rebellion, for many, is merely a search for their own identity, an identity that is not easily carved out by parents who allow their children to do as they please. For healthy self-esteem to grow there ought to be a partnership between the child and the parent in which the parameters for a healthy functioning relationship are clearly seen.

Democratic parenting

This is a more balanced approach to parenting in which children are allowed to be independent thinkers and encouraged to take responsibility for their actions. From an early age they are encouraged to share in decisions that are made around the home. They are enabled to develop team-sharing skills and to make their own choices within certain defined boundaries. These boundaries are not rigid but allow for flexibility. Discipline is carried out with a sense of affection and caring and children have a clear sense of what they are being punished for. The emphasis is not so much on punishment as it is on reward. Mistakes are seen as teaching opportunities and not as occasions to berate the child or to call him demeaning names.

Of all the parenting styles I believe this is the best environment in which a healthy self-esteem can be nurtured in children. There is a sense of openness which creates an atmosphere of sharing. This minimizes fear as children are encouraged to speak freely about their concerns. They do not have to worry that their views do not matter or that they will be put down for what they say. It is important that children have free access to their parents; where there can be free exchange of conversation between parents and child. If they cannot go to the parents, to whom shall they go? Should they go to the drug pusher on the corner, to the peer who might have been exposed to the brutality of autocratic parenting? Or should they go to the adult whose life has already been derailed and who are now on the prowl seeking other lives to wreck? Children need the protection stability and moral force that a caring parent should provide.

Neglectful parenting

This is very similar to laissez-faire parenting except that in neglectful parenting, the parents simply do not care what happens to the child. The parent will provide the basic necessities that are necessary for survival such as food, clothing and shelter-and sometimes they do so poorly. But, beyond this, there is no active involvement with the child, no serious concern to teach them what is necessary to develop healthy values and attitudes toward life.

With this approach it is not difficult to see that children in this parenting environment are likely to grow up without a sense of responsibility. They are pretty much on their own and some children have to fend for themselves. As they grow older they are forced to take on adult roles to which they are not suited. This is not fair to them. Every child has a right to enjoy his or her childhood, to be able to play, frolic and just be a child. When that childhood is circumscribed by the child having to assume adult roles at an early age because they are neglected by their parents, psychological problems can develop. I have often heard adults in therapy express with great distress that they never had a childhood or that they had to grow up too fast. Low self-esteem is often seen in neglected children. This can lead to a host of behavioral problems.

In conclusion, the choice of any style or combination of styles is the parents' choice. From my experience, both in growing my own kids and from what I have observed in so many home situations, the environment in which healthy self-esteem can best grow and thrive is one in which there is a great amount of respect, love and gratitude shown by the parent to the child and the child to the parent. It is about establishing a bond of affection, based on unconditional love, which can instill a sense of responsibility and love for humanity in children. It is one in which the child can ask questions without feeling that he or she will be put down. It is one in which the parent is a facilitator and mentor and not one who revels in a command and control approach which intrudes into every aspect of the child's life.

Ask yourself these questions as we close out this section:

In which of the parenting styles mentioned above do you believe you were brought up?

How has this affected your self-esteem?

If you are a parent which of these styles do you believe you are using to grow your children, or if they are already grown, which style do you believe you used in growing them?

If you answer these questions seriously and honestly you may discover something that you never knew about yourself or your child before. You have affected your child's life in more profound ways than you may be aware of. Hug them, love them and let them feel very special, no matter how old they are.

CHAPTER THREE

BULLYING AND THE PROBLEM OF SELF-ESTEEM

I have included this chapter on bullying not only because it is directly related to the problem of self-esteem but because it has become a more intense problem in recent times with an increasing number of children committing suicide. Bullying is not just a problem for parents and the young; it has become a societal problem. My intention here is to continue to raise awareness about it and hopefully motivate others to become more involved in eliminating it from our communities.

We may start by defining what bullying is. Simply put, it is the use of power to intimidate, control and cause harm and embarrassment to others, usually those who are considered to be weak and who can be singled out for this kind of action. It is a deliberate action on the part of the bully that is repeated on the person or group being bullied. Bullying is carried out in various ways:

1   Verbal-by name-calling and teasing. This is not just assigning a nickname to someone, but calling the person derogatory names, especially when the person has indicated that he or she does not like it. The fact the person does not like it spurs on the

bully who derives pleasure from the person's seeming inability to defend himself.

2   Physical-by hitting, shoving or pushing. Physical contacts like these may appear to be harmless but they can turn quite ugly, particularly when there is a crowd to cheer on the bully. This can result in grievous bodily harm, as we have seen in far too many instances. Such behavior can lead to serious legal consequences.

3   Social-This is done through spreading rumors about someone or by deliberately ostracizing a person from a social group or a group of friends, thus resulting in the breakup of friendships and relation-ships. The isolated person is often subject to taunts which reinforce the idea that he or she does not belong to that group or is not welcomed there.

4   Cyber or digital bullying-This is where the internet (through social media such as Facebook and YouTube), cell phones (through texting and sexting messaging) are used to intimidate and harass per-sons. This form of bullying has become very vicious in recent times and is responsible for the spike in suicides among young people. These technological marvels are potent tools in the hands of a bully because they are able to carry out their activities with a certain degree of anonymity. They can do so whenever and wherever they wish. In many in-stances, by the time they are caught, their harmful behavior would have already had its toll on the hapless victim.

Whatever form bullying takes it should have become quite clear by now that it is not a harmless, random prank that someone selfishly indulges in to bring pleasure to himself. As we have seen it can have deadly consequences. Suicides are the extreme forms of these consequences, but youngsters who have been bullies or have been bullied can suffer from certain psychological deficits that follow them into adulthood. Some people never outgrow the effects of bullying. The bullies grow up with negative self-concepts which can be seen in the way they treat others, whether as a demanding tyrant at the workplace when they are given charge over others or a dictatorial spouse or parent who drives fear in the household. It is the lasting scars of bullying that can have the most crippling effects on the emotional health of people and which can be the cause of their biggest setbacks in life. Bullying does not only kill physically, but emotionally and spiritually.

Helping our children to deal with bullying

Not every child has the coping skills to deal with bullying and this applies both to the bully and the bullied. Children who are already operating with low mental deficits are especially vulnerable and are likely to become easy targets for bullies. When they are picked on or set upon, their already fragile self-esteem cannot deal with the onslaught and they are driven to the edge. Children can be quite brutal with each other. They do not often realize that what might be a prank or joke to them can hurt another person deeply. If an adult feels embarrassed, troubled or harassed by other adults' relentless taunts, he has recourse in the law courts and can get the matter dealt with judiciously.

33

Children also have recourse in law, but how many of those being harassed and taunted think about this? Further, how many parents act to stop this harassment before it is too late? What seems to be the prevailing reaction of children who are being bullied is that they internalize their hurts and in time crawl into a dark world from which some of them never emerge. They suffer in silence as they do not believe they have anyone in whom they can confide- not their parents, not the guidance counselor at school, not even the pastor in the local church.

Charles Blow, a columnist at the *New York Times*, recalled the time when he was bullied as an eight year old child. He decided to end his life after he had crawled into the "security" of his dark world. He felt ridiculed and ostracized and in this dark, lonely place as he described it, he became desperate and confused. In that state he was saved from personal tragedy by the recollection of the voice of his mother singing.

In an earlier separate blog entry entitled *Two Little Boys*, (*New York Times*, April 24, 2009) Blow wrote about two boys in different parts of the country who had committed suicide after being relentlessly taunted as homosexuals. He wrote:

> Children can't see their budding lives through the long lens of wisdom...For them,, the weight of ridicule and ostracism can feel crushing and without the possibility of reprieve. And, in that dark and lonely place, desperate and confused, they can make horrible decisions that can't be undone.

The question that should haunt every parent is whether his or her child has crawled into that lonely place. They can only know the answer to this question by being vigilant and by talking constantly with their kids, whether there are signs of bullying or not. It cannot be more stressed how important parents are to the issue of bullying. Bullies and their victims come from homes. Unhealthy home environments where children are not exposed to positive, unconditional love can be breeding grounds for bullies. They can also breed conditions where children grow up with low self-esteem, which can make them uniquely vulnerable to the tactics of the bully.

Parents ought to be more aware of their responsibilities both in preventing their children from becoming bullies as well as defending and protecting them when they come under attack from bullies. As we noted in a previous chapter, children live in a controlled environment and ought to be subject to the discipline and love of their parents. Parents should be able to detect the tell-tale signs that indicate that something is wrong, either in the aggressive or hostile behavior of the child or in him being withdrawn, getting poor grades, not sleeping and being sickly. These are not necessarily signs that your child is a bully or is being bullied, but being aware can help you converse with your child and uncover what may be happening to them on a regular basis. Bullying does not happen in isolation.

Parents should not be afraid to take resolute action when their children come under attack from bullies. This applies further to teachers and school administrators who are sometimes tardy or negligent in addressing bullying with the seriousness they should. This is regrettable, for teachers are often the first responders, so to speak, who have to come to the defense of the bullied child. A teacher or any adult for that matter, cannot ignore bullying or just shrug it off as "kids just being kids." Every report of bullying ought to be investigated by school authorities and where there is credible evidence of bullying immediate action must be taken to prevent and end it.

Part of the preventative measures that can be taken can be to have more courses on self-respect and self-esteem taught in our schools from pre-k to grade 12. These are subjects that should become integral to every school curriculum in these grades. For, if the home is not providing for this, the school has to be the secondary source for the transmission of the values that lead to healthy self-esteem. You hardly hear of children committing suicide because they fail to do their math or science. But they do so in increasingly frightening numbers if they think poorly of themselves and if the taunts and jeers of their peers push them into an abyss.

The federal government is considering legislation to crack down on cyber bullying. A number of states have already implemented legislation to outlaw communication intended to intimidate, harass or coerce. This is so especially with regard to gay, lesbian, bisexual and transgender bullying which have picked up pace in recent times. It is good to see the government stepping in, as this demonstrates greater awareness of the problem and shows attempts are being made to address it. But, just as laws against drunk driving do not prevent intoxicated people from driving on the road, laws against bullying will not end the scourge anytime soon. It will take the collective resources of the community-home, school, church and other civic organizations- to bear on the problem.

We cannot become concerned only when the problem affects us directly. The attitude that some people seem to have is that if their child is not involved it is not their problem. This must change. It is our entire problem; one child lost to suicide because of bullying is one child too many. It really does take a village to end bullying, as we know it today. In the end it comes down to how much we love them unconditionally and how we care for them. Both the bully and the bullied are crying out to be loved, to be hugged, to be affirmed, not ostracized or ridiculed. We must help them to appreciate the difference they see in other children so that they too can develop a positive and healthy concept of themselves. Children who have a positive self-esteem do not go around bullying others. Neither will they crumble under the weight of a bully.

Questions:
When was the last time you hugged your child and told him that you love him?
Is your child special?

CHAPTER FOUR

SEVEN EFFECTIVE WAYS TO BUILD AND MAINTAIN HIGH SELF-ESTEEM

We have come to what I would regard as the most important chapter of the book: that of building and maintaining high self-esteem. As we noted earlier, self-esteem cannot be earned, but has to be worked at. I believe by now you will agree with me that self-esteem is not an abstract concept, but one that is very real and which has profound implications for how we live our lives from day to day. For as Nathaniel Branden noted in his book, *The Psychology of Self-esteem*, there can be no value judgment more important or more decisive in man's psychological development and motivation, than the estimate he passes on himself. This estimate or value, to repeat, is something that each person has to arrive at on their own. The home, school, church, institutions in society, friends and even enemies may help him in arriving at this estimate, but in the end he has to take responsibility for this himself. How he does and the conclusions he draws, are critical to his peace of mind and his success in life.

The whole idea behind self-esteem is that we can live positive and more fulfilling lives. If we are experiencing low self-esteem because we have lost our job or because we feel deflated by what people are saying about us, I believe we will be helped by the seven effective ways that I have mentioned here. I will caution that those who experience high self-esteem or who have seen this as the state that best defines them, should not become too narcissistic or self-absorbed by this which can be easy to do. I am speaking here about genuine high self-esteem, not the arrogance that parades itself as a virtue and to which everyone that comes into contact with should bow. I am sure the head of a drug cartel will convince himself that he has garnered all his wealth by having high self-esteem. This might be supreme self-confidence or narcissism, but not self-esteem in the sense of which we have defined it in this book. A high self-esteem should serve humanity, not hurt or degrade it.

If we can train our lives to achieve a state of high self-esteem then we do not have to worry too much about low self-esteem, which events in our lives will throw at us from time to time. The person who is abiding in or functioning at a high level of self-esteem will take these events in stride. If they are called ugly they know that there is something deep down inside of them that makes them beautiful no matter what the world may say. If someone tries to vilify them or put them down they know that they do not have to rely on anyone for validation. They would have worked through their own self-doubts and have developed the strength of character that now allows them to be self confident and to stand tall. In the midst of adversity they have developed the emotional resilience to forge ahead and to retain their sanity when others around them are losing theirs.

The factors that I have set out below are not exhaustive of the many ways that one can build and maintain high self-esteem. I have found that they work for me and they come out of my own experience along with having to work with people over the years who have suffered low self-esteem issues even to the point of depression and entertaining suicidal thoughts. That is why I know that self-esteem is not an abstract or isolated issue but goes to the depth of the practical realities that confront each of our lives from day to day. In suggesting these factors my interest is neither clinical nor academic. There are many books that abound with this subject and anyone can consult them if they want to pursue the subjects along these lines. I have tried to suggest practical realities born out of experience with the hope that we may all look at self-esteem in perhaps a new and more determined way, a way that impacts our lives. There are things we may want to change or not change. Again, and as always, the verdict is up to each of us.

1. **Avoid being a perfectionist**. Many people associate high self-esteem with perfection. A perfectionist does not believe in making mistakes. They hold themselves to very high standards and become very upset when they do not achieve excellence in what they do. They do not only demand high standards for themselves but set them for other people. They find it difficult to get on with those who cannot meet these high standards and so they either become demanding or isolate themselves socially from people. By imposing a high demand on themselves, by setting higher and higher standards, perfectionists tend to

work themselves to a frazzle to prove that they can achieve and thus gain acceptance.

Perfectionism is not itself a disease or recognized disorder, but it can indicate the presence of disorders such as compulsive disorders. Striving to be perfect can also lead to other disorders such as mood and anxiety issues. The perfectionist has made himself a prisoner of a certain set of beliefs from which he ought to be freed. He is a prisoner of his own misshapen view of reality that is in urgent need of transformation and healing.

Perfectionism is never an indication of high self-esteem because however high a value we place on our lives none of us will ever be able to do everything perfectly. We can strive to do and to be the best we can but there are times when we will fall short. The perfectionist of course believes that he must not or cannot fall short, and therein lies the tragedy that often befalls such persons. This may explain why the perfectionist is so afraid of criticisms. Yet, the harder they work at being perfect, the more ammunition they give to their critics to criticize them.

On the other hand, people with high self-esteem are highly motivated individuals. They will work hard for what they want and set high standards for themselves. They believe in excellence but they do not cross the fine line in believing in the divinity of such excellence. Therefore, they will accept constructive criticisms if they fail to attain the high standards they have set. Whining, complaining and being grumpy are not options for them. They do not have to be perfect to prove their worth and pity the person who believes that they should be. The perfectionist, however, will blame and belittle himself, while at the same time not recognizing the insane and humanly impossible standards he has set.

The highly motivated person will understand the value of flexibility. If one thing does not work, he tries another. If one door closes he goes in search for another that might be open. It might be open to a different set of possibilities but he walks into the open room willing and ready to take on the challenges that present themselves. He will confront his fears and resist the impulse to quit. While he may fail today, he believes that the sun will rise tomorrow.

2. **We must accept ourselves for who we are. We alone can live in our own skin.** These or variations of these statements are things that most of us say to people from time to time. They are often said in a glib manner as most of the time we do not know enough about the person to truthfully tell him to accept himself as he is. When you are tempted to say these words to someone, ask yourself this question: What am I really asking the person to accept? If the person is an alcoholic or drug abuser, a child abuser, a perpetrator or a victim of domestic violence or some other negative characteristic, would you be telling him to accept himself for who he is? If you had knowledge of the person's behavior would you hope that he would change and then move on to self-acceptance?

Self-acceptance is not easy. For some people it comes after a lifetime of epic struggle to love themselves, to feel good about themselves at least most of the time and to find affirmation and meaning in their daily work. For some it comes after years of painful rejection, of being told that they would not amount to anything much. Children who have been demeaned and neglected will find it hard to come to a point of self-acceptance. They grow up frightened and empty with a sickening feeling of loneliness in a crowded world. So, too, are people who have been abused mentally or physically. They develop an interior sense of worthlessness and carry around personal wounds that have not been healed.

This is why I stated earlier that it may not be appropriate to tell people to just simply accept themselves because we often do not know what people are going through, what wounds are still open in their lives and to what extent their lives have been scarred by the blows that life has thrown at them. But, there comes a point at which we have to realize that change has to take place and the extent to which that will happen will depend on us summoning up the will to take the first step. To where? This is the hard question for there are often many voices of contradiction screaming in our ears and we have to determine which one we are going to listen to. Of one thing we are certain: we cannot continue with the status quo that our life has thrown up and neither can we continue being what the world is telling us to be. Our happiness, peace of mind, purpose and destiny all depend on us finding comfort in our own skin, for there is really nowhere else to go.

Many people lose a sense of who they are and end up failing in life by simply buying into what other people tell them that they are. But one's worth as a person, which they have to finally come to accept, cannot be defined by how others think about them, but what they think about themselves. Self-acceptance begins with the realization that we cannot live our lives as other people want us to live them. We have to be aware of our own strengths and weaknesses and get the help that we need to reconcile them in the context of our own life so we can be motivated to work on the desired changes, which we ourselves alone can affirm.

Steve Jobs, the Apple co-founder who died recently, was not important only for the gadgets he invented. He too had a rocky start in life starting with being rejected at birth. His biography by Walter Isaacson, (*Steve Jobs*), shows a life of great contrasts but mirrored the restlessness of a man who struggled to find meaning in his life to the very end. Like all of us must, he had to come to terms with his impending death. Samuel Johnson, the British author and critic, once quipped at the impending death of an Anglican clergyman by hanging, that when a man faces death it concentrates his mind wonderfully (*Life of Samuel Johnson, by James Boswell*). And so it does.

In perhaps the most important speech he ever delivered, Steve Jobs in his commencement address at Stanford University in 2005, told his audience some important truths about life and about self-validation. He said:

> Your time is limited, so don't waste it living someone else's life. Don't be trapped by dogma- which is living with the results of other people's thinking. Don't let the noise of others' opinions drown out your inner voice. And most important, have the courage to follow your heart and intention. They somehow already know what you truly want to become. Everything else is secondary.

45

What I believe Jobs was saying in a most profound way is try to live a life of authenticity, not waiting around for the approval of others. Make the best of your God-given potentials to realize your dreams knowing that life is not in the business of dishing out free lunches. We alone can affirm the best for ourselves. There are times when we may have to break off sticks in our ears so that we can hear our own voices for a change. It is a person with poor self-esteem who constantly listens to what other people tell them before they can step boldly into the future that beckons. I am not saying that we should not listen to advice, but I have come to know an important thing about advice: it can only be given within the context of the giver's personal limitations and some people can be very limited in what they are advising. I know lives that have been wrecked because they followed bad advice. I also know lives that have been wrecked because they failed to follow good advice. But as Jobs said, time is limited. Do not waste it trying to live someone else's life.

3. **Accept responsibility for our own actions**. This may sound simplistic because one would expect that this should be the case, but it is surprising how rarely people accept responsibility for the things they say or do. Accepting responsibility and being accountable for ones actions is one of the most important ways to build and sustain high self-esteem. The people with low self-esteem will constantly give excuses for their behavior or blame other people and events for things that happen in their lives. We will never gain self- acceptance by doing this.

Accepting responsibility means a willingness to be personally accountable for what we do. This is important especially when we consider that to every action there is a consequence and often these consequences are unintended. They can have a far reaching impact on a person's life and those around him. Ask Bernie Madoff.

Accepting personal responsibility is not readily done for to do so one has to be prepared to face the consequences of one's actions. People who are adept at shrugging off responsibility become good practitioners in the art of projection and deceit. Being unwilling to face the consequences of their words or actions, they have to lie their way out of situations or find someone who can take the fall for them, someone they can blame for what they have done or what they have become in life or failed to become. The tactic is as old as Adam's hiding under Eve's skirt (fig leaf) and blaming her for having given him the forbidden fruit, to the child breaking the vase and blaming his sister for the action. This happens in every sphere of life.

There is a saying that misery loves company and I have come to see that this is a true statement. We must be on the lookout for the person who lives irresponsibly and who will suck us into the vortex of the misery caused by his own irresponsible approach to life. If we allow them they will pull us into their own chaotic world and before we know it we begin to fail as they have failed. It is hard for us to have worked hard to make something of our lives simply to have them wrecked by the irresponsibility of others. And, some people who have become quite adept at deception can ruin our well manicured lives in a short time. I have seen this in countless marriages. I never cease to be amazed why a promising man or woman should think that by marrying an irresponsible person they can transform him or her into the most beautiful and loving person ever. This may work in fairy tale books but it certainly does not work in real life.

Another area where people are tempted to accept responsibility for others is in the home where parents sometimes think they have to pick up the slack for an errant child. Let me clarify that I am not here speaking of boomerang kids, that is, young graduates who have left college or university and for some reason, economic or otherwise, have had to return to their nests at their parents' home. Some have found that the nest is not the same as they left it after high school. There are fewer feathers and even a little more thorns than they expected. The truth is that whatever the state of the nest the recession has hit home hard for many of these kids. Their self-esteem is under great pressure as they are finding it hard to adjust to the economic realities that face them. They were grown to consider themselves special and many of them have worked hard and equipped themselves in a way that they should not be denied the essential things of living an honorable and even prosperous life. Now they find themselves at home; what might have appeared to be a temporary arrangement for many is turning out to be something more permanent as the recessionary winds persist. What this is calling for is a new set of parenting skills as parents seek to adjust to this reality. Many are not coping because they are neither equipped nor accustomed to the demands that this new reality is placing upon them. A lot of patience is cautioned as parents meander around these demands.

In the context also of parents helping out their children, I am not referring to children who have faced some temporary hardships and setbacks in life and have to return home to sort themselves out. This happens to both men and women but in my experience women figure more prominently in this regard. A number of women and perhaps to a lesser extent men, go back home after a failed relationship or marriage. Life can be rather unkind to us and there should never be a time when a home should not be a safe haven to those who come in from the storm. Those who do so need a temporary shelter in which to sort themselves out. The wise parent will not judge them or berate them as failures, but will provide support and wise counsel which will help them build up their self-esteem until they can face the world again. Children who are so helped ought to accept that such arrangements can only be temporary. Their parents too have their lives to live, however glad they may be to have the child at home.

My concern is with children who have been given a chance in life by parents who worked hard to see them through but who simply wasted their parents' substance and now look to their parents to continue picking up behind them. Yes, I hear the protestation from those who would regard themselves as the prodigal son, but it should not be forgotten that the son did not go back home to be a burden to the household, but to be a hired servant and so earn his keep. A good parent will always find love for a child, but a good parent should not be expected to be burdened by a child who fails to take responsibility for his or her life. It is bad enough for parents to assume responsibility for the actions and negative behavior of grown children, but it is infinitely worse when the grandparents get pulled into the picture. Expecting constant bailouts from a parent or grandparent when we are healthy enough to look out for ourselves is hardly a way of living a respectable life governed by self-esteem. Parents who enable their healthy children to do this are not being of any help to them. What they are doing is contributing to the demise of their self-esteem. There is a point at which a parent, guardian or grandparent has to draw the line in the sand and declare enough is enough and remove the crutch. This is called tough love which is not always easy but which has to be done to restore balance in a situation that has all the resemblances of chaos. The parent that does this lovingly may save a life; they will certainly place that child on the road to building high self-esteem.

Drug addiction, whose responsibility?

Another area which I will only mention briefly is that of drug addiction or substance abuse. As one trained in the area of family therapy, I can well appreciate how difficult and complex the problem of drug addiction is and how much of a nightmare it has become for families that have had to deal with loved ones exposed to it. The problem cannot be trivialized or broken down to one common denominator of irresponsibility. There are many factors which drive a person to abuse drugs and this happens in every social and economic strata of society. My intention here is not to judge or apportion blame but to highlight the fact that in every expression of negative behavior that can do great harm to persons, someone has to accept responsibility for the behavior or the lifestyle. This is especially so when you consider how grave a threat the drug problem has become for America. It is now no longer a personal problem that wrecks families but is deemed a serious national security threat. The savage drug wars on the US-Mexican border have brought this threat into sharp focus.

Although the Substance Abuse and Mental Health Services Administration (SAMSHA) has reported a decline in the use of hard drugs in various categories, drug addiction and its attendant problems still pose a risk to communities, to families, to productivity at the workplace and to health and criminal justice costs, in general. Prescription drug abuse has become the fastest growing drug problem in America and has been described as an epidemic by the Center for Disease Control and Prevention. The State of Florida alone dispenses more prescription drugs than all the other 49 combined. Prescription drug abuse is the leading cause of death for people between the ages of 18-35. This is staggering on the face of it. Singularly, America accounts for the survival and maintenance of the global multi-billion dollar drug trade. Put another way, more drugs flow into the United States than into any other country on the planet. This is an inconvenient truth that any nation would want to dodge, but this is the reality.

Rather than trying to evade reality, it would be more prudent to ask the uncomfortable questions as to why there is such an appetite for drugs in the country and why there is this huge craving to escape reality through substance abuse. The answers to these questions are obviously not easy, but they have to be asked. One of the reasons for the failure of American drug policy over the years is that there has been a greater emphasis placed on the supply side of the equation than the demand. We have concentrated our efforts on stopping drugs coming into the country while ignoring any real emphasis on the demand side, that is, why there is such a huge hunger for drugs. It is on the demand side that personal responsibility for one's action is best seen. By economic logic, if there is a fall in demand there would be a corresponding fall in supply.

Every American that uses an illegal drug must be told that he or she is contributing to the demise of America. Directly or indirectly he or she is contributing to every sale that is made and every gun that is exchanged for drugs. Furthermore, they are unwitting accomplices in the corruption of national institutions and the undermining of law and order in the society. They are contributors to the wrecking of families and the cauterization of the promise of our young. They must be educated to the alternatives and other forms of therapeutic interventions that are available if they see themselves headed down a road of addiction. Government policy must be aimed increasingly toward supporting such programs with grants. The president must lend the power of his office to these programs and to encouraging people to seek help where necessary. Finally, drug education must become a viable part of the curriculum of our schools starting from grade 8 to grade 12. These are not panaceas that will cause the problem of drug addiction to disappear but they are steps in the right direction in helping to stem the demand for illicit drugs. It is time that we all become addicted to the truth, however inconvenient, of the danger that we all face from the illicit drug trade.

Another area of lacking responsibility for our actions is in the political realm. One of the reasons why our political situation is so messed up is that there are men and women in power who have lost sense of the moral responsibility to govern. Both sides blame each other for the failures of government without recognizing that the fault lies in their own outdated and skewed ideological approach to governance. People who behave like this, whether in government, the school, the church, the home, or any other area of life are cowards at heart.

The person with high self-esteem recognizes that it takes a force of will to own up for what he has done. No amount of justification or excuses will suffice. He realizes that the more he practices accepting responsibility the better he feels about himself and the stronger his decision-making powers. He will grow in confidence because he will be holding himself to the high bar of accountability. A life that is not accountable to itself is hardly worth living for it will constantly be in search for someone or something to blame.

4. **Develop a strong moral center for our lives**. This is closely allied to the practice of personal accountability. A person who is not able to have moral clarity between right and wrong will find it difficult holding himself accountable for anything. Neither will he be willing to have anyone hold him accountable. If there is ever a time when we need to have moral clarity about the things we do or say the time is now. In every sphere of human endeavor we are living in a time of moral crisis evidenced largely in people's inability to distinguish clearly between right and wrong.

53

We are in an age where people act more on how and what they feel than from a deep interior sense of whether an action or statement is right or wrong, correct or false.

In a recent article entitled, *If it Feels Right*, *New York Times* columnist David Brooks commented on an interesting study done by noted Notre Dame sociologist, Christian Smith, on the lack of moral clarity among Americans between the ages of 18-23. Smith found that when asked about a moral dilemma they had faced, about two-thirds could not explain what a moral dilemma was or gave answers that were not moral at all. Some thought that driving drunk or cheating in school were not considered to be moral concerns or that moral choices were just a matter of individual tastes. Very significantly, right and wrong were related to individual tastes and how one feels.

The study merely confirms what has been an emerging trend over the past two decades that acting morally is just about how one feels. The thinking seems to be: if it feels good do it, if it does not then don't or wait until you feel up to it. People who have worked hard at coming to a high value of themselves know almost instinctively that one cannot rely on mere feelings to determine right and wrong. They are able to make a clear distinction between the two categories, knowing that their actions can severely impact the lives of others. They seek out truth and when they find it they stand on the strength of their convictions. They know that we either accept the truth or reject it. If we reject it, the factual foundations upon which it stands remain. It does not remove this foundation on which it stands. Neither does it remove the consequences that may result. So the person who seeks to have a high value for his life will always seek to speak the truth whatever the costs.

A lot of wrong has been done on Wall Street by the seeming unwillingness of people to seek the truth and live by it. We have all witnessed the inevitable consequences of bad behavior. As far as I can determine, the economic crisis that the world is going through has one common denominator: the abandonment of a sense of morality in our financial decision-making processes. These processes have been corrupted by the insatiable desire for profit at all costs. It does not matter if millions of people lose their homes or their jobs or their very lives in the process. What is important is that money be made and if a recession is the result we will not waste a good recession but will milk it to make even more profits. This seems to be the thinking of many in the financial sector who do not even want to have their activities regulated. Leave it to the good consciences of people and they will do the right thing. Well, we have seen the tragedy of this kind of philosophy.

One thing that our business and financial schools cannot teach us is how to develop a viable conscience that has the other person at the center of our concern. Methodologies that are taught in some of our more important schools such as Harvard Business School or the Wharton School of Finance are not necessarily reliable guides to developing a clear and clean conscience. Even business courses on ethics are made subservient to the larger questions of the profit motive and sustaining shareholder value. Driven by an insatiable appetite to make money creative accounting can be done to drive the value of a particular stock. The tragedies of Enron, MCI, Tyco and others did not happen in a vacuum. They happened in situations where the voice of conscience was drowned to satisfy the expediency of profit at all costs.

Yet, we cannot live happily or successfully if we ignore the voice of conscience. As a principle of self-regulation it is placed within us for a purpose. If we fail to be regulated by it the arms of the state will step in to regulate it for us, and even to save us from ourselves and others from us. There are certain lines which if we cross will lead us into perilous waters and will severely impair our relationship with others. Persons with high self-esteem have a strong sense of moral obligation to others and so put a check on their behavior so that they do not trespass on the sacred space of other people. In developing a moral center for your life ask yourself this question: Of what is your conscience afraid?

5. Stand on the strength of our convictions but know when to yield. A person with strong self-esteem stands on the strength of his convictions. He does not profess to know everything neither does he believe he is a perfection-ist. He knows what he believes in and will stand his ground until he is convinced otherwise. One of the worst persons anyone can come across is someone who does not know what he believes in, and therefore, bends to every wind of thought or doctrine that blows his way, never taking a position on anything. Like some politicians, he puts his finger in the air to determine in which direction the wind is blowing and then goes off in that direction.

People who have suffered from low self-esteem, especially over a prolonged period, often find themselves in this kind of situation. Instead of taking a stance on some issue, they will speak through another person's voice instead of their own. Their fear is to be confronted on what is being said, for they know that deep down they do not have the integrity to defend that in which they claim belief. Like him or dislike him, this is one of the reasons that Herman Cain surged in the Republican presidential primaries, despite the allegations of sexual misconduct against him. He defied the primary elections' political conventions and stated what he believed in. People admired his willingness to stand up for his convictions even though they might not have agreed with his position on issues.

When we hold steadfastly to what we believe in we are likely to be called arrogant or stubborn. There are people who are threatened by others who have a great deal of confidence in themselves and who believe steadfastly in the integrity of their positions. Weaker personalities can cringe in the presence of such persons. Instead of cringing there may be something to learn from or emulate in such persons. I am known to hold almost stubbornly to my convictions. I will defend my convictions vigorously. I do so because I do not come to my conviction about issues casually or superficially. I do not believe what I believe simply because people tell me that this is how it ought to be. Throughout my school life I was argumentative because I did not simply believe something because it was written in a book or because a teacher or professor said so.

But, I have also learnt over the years that there is dignity in yielding one's positions. I cannot be right on all matters. No one can be. It is only a fool who holds tenaciously to a position against which he has been convinced. Sometimes it is pride that causes us to hold on for dear life when it is clearly prudent to let go. I once saw a western movie which portrayed a quintessential battle between the white settlers and the Indians in eighteenth-century America. Cochise, the head of the Apache tribe in the late 1800's, conferred together with other chiefs to work out a peace treaty with the white soldiers. They were not far in the discussions and yet some of the chiefs wanted to end it and leave. Cochise went to one of those who was leaving and said to him, by paraphrase: "when a tree is caught in a storm, if it does not bend it will be taken up by its roots." This has stayed with me and I wonder how many people have been taken up by their roots by their unwillingness to bend, to yield, to stand down for a more opportune time.

A person with high self-esteem has mastered this art of yielding. He knows when to give up something to get something. There are times when we have to step off the high horse of pride to the donkey of humility to win the day. This does not mean weakness or an abandonment of one's position, but shows maturity and prudence. Stubborn commitment to a faded idea or one that has died on the vines is no way to win friends and influence people. Neither is this a clear path to success. People with high self-esteem know this.

6. **Build emotional resilience**. Self-esteem does not grow in a vacuum but is the product of negative or positive emotions that drive our thinking or acting. Positive or negative emotions help us to deal with reality. The extent to which we are able to deal successfully with the daily realities of

life that confront us will depend upon the level of emotional resilience we have built up over time.

Emotional resilience basically is one's ability to deal creatively and successfully with difficult situations that arise from day to day. The ability to do so is best seen in crisis situations or situations of great stress where the person's ability to cope is put under a severe test. The person who is operating from a level of low self-esteem is likely to show less resilience and may more easily crumble under the weight of the presenting problem. Conversely, the person with high self-esteem will show a higher degree of resilience as he would have developed effective coping mechanisms over time that will assist him to ride out the crisis. The more emotionally resilient you are the higher the level of your self-esteem is likely to be and the less resilient you are emotionally the lower the level of your self-esteem.

The important thing then is to strive towards building strong emotional resilience. Like anything worth having, this can only be accomplished by hard work. Strong emotional resilience does not arrive at our doorsteps like a UPS package overnight. It is something that has to be worked on and once achieved will stay with you. What are some of the ways in which we can develop strong emotional resilience? I will mention a few here.

We must work towards healing past hurts in our lives. Life can be quite brutal and it can leave us with wounds that are very difficult to heal. Physical wounds will heal over time but the most difficult ones to heal are emotional. Even when we have gotten over emotional pain there may be what I call the "scarring of the soul" which asserts itself to remind us that it is not over yet. Yet, a way has to be found to achieve emotional healing by which a person is able to achieve personal harmony and contentment by employing emotions to achieve positive outcomes. None of this is easy and professional help might have to be sought by the person who is burdened by past hurts, whatever the nature and origin of those hurts. The past is important only to the extent that it sits in the present and wreaks havoc like a bull in a store of fine crockery. This is precisely the description of what past hurts and brokenness can do to a person's life: wreak havoc and destroy the beautiful crockery they once had. We alone must summon the courage to put an end to this carnage. As soon as we have set our lives on this course we will begin to feel better about ourselves. As time transpires we will slowly build resilience as our self-esteem is restored. But we have to take action.

We should not allow anyone to push our buttons. People with low self-esteem often allow others to push them around or to generally exploit their weaknesses. People who exploit other people's weaknesses often do so without thinking; others do so deliberately and in keeping with their own disfigured personalities. There are a lot of emotionally wounded people walking around seeking new victims. Their hero is Sad Sack, the *Harvey Comics* fictional character who endured all kinds of humiliations in army life and walked around with a sad countenance. If you tell those kinds of people good morning they are likely to ask you what is so good about the morning. There is a saying that misery loves company and there are people who are prepared to mess up our lives if we allow them to do so. They will pull us into their own chaotic world. They will sow weeds in our carefully manicured lawn. Nothing will please them more than to know that our lives are just as messy as theirs. We alone have the power to prevent this and so we have to be strong and know how and when to respond to such people when they try to press our buttons. Part of building resilience then, is cultivating the power of saying no, of knowing what battles to fight and how to fight them, and of knowing which friendships to walk away from and which to keep. No one can push our buttons unless we allow them.

Develop a "locus of control." The term "locus of control" was developed by psychologists to determine whether people feel that they have control over their own lives or whether they are controlled by external forces over which they have little or no control. People with a strong internal locus of control generally feel happy about themselves because they believe that they have the power to determine the course of their lives. They generally live healthier lives as they are not prone to worry, self-defeating thoughts or depression. Their attitude to living is not determined by what others say about them but by their own strong sense of who they are. It is not that their lives are unaffected by external events. All our lives are. But, they are not unduly influenced by these events. Those with an external locus of control are the complete opposite of all this. They are easily overwhelmed by their circumstances and are likely to blame other people for their misfortunes or for their inability to cope with what life throws at them. They are prone to health problems such as anxiety disorders, depression and other difficulties produced by stress. There is professional help available for people who find themselves in this situation. Again, it is up to the person to seek help and this can begin by just confiding in someone they respect who can help in getting the intervention one needs.

Exercise, exercise, and then meditate. The relevance of exercise to the whole matter of building self-esteem and resilience can be easily taken for granted and overlooked. Yet, many have recognized that there can be no more powerful tool to de-clutter the mind and build right attitudes than exercise and, I would add, exercise accompanied by meditation. By exercise and meditation I do not mean elaborate and expensive programs that people often indulge in to give the impression that they take personal fitness seriously. The fitness industry has become increasingly expensive for this reason. People speak of "exercise regimens" as if these are ends in themselves and as if they can be miraculous cures to a lot of the things that ail us. This may be good for many people, and if they find this approach helpful, then so be it. I am more concerned about the less formalized approach to exercise; the simple matter of taking a brisk walk, light jog or bike ride through the park or the neighborhood. The value of gardening must not be underestimated as this allows for bending and stretching which you may not get in other forms of exercising. I like gardening best because apart from good exercise, you reap the added benefits of what you plant and you feel at one with nature and with your spiritual self. I believe that exercise followed by meditation relaxes the mind and allows you to concentrate on deep things of the spirit. Again, the emphasis on meditation does not have to be about any elaborate system of yoga or other type of trained meditational program. It can be as simple as just sitting down, closing our eyes, coming to a place of stillness and concentrating our minds on a subject of significance. We can do this right after completing our exercise activity. This is even more effective when followed by a soothing bath. Do this often enough and we will build resilience. Our endorphins will see to it.

7. **We must celebrate our significance**. Celebrating our significance means, among other things, tapping into our spiritual energy and recognizing our importance to the world. How significant we believe we are will determine the level of self-esteem at which we operate. Our pursuit of happiness will ultimately depend upon whether we believe in our own significance. I am not talking about a self-serving narcissism where people become obsessed with an inflated sense of their own importance to the exclusion of everyone else around them. Where they are the only people that matter and where there is the grandiose sense that without them the world cannot function. The cemeteries of the world are filled with the bones of people who thought and behaved like this and the world has not ended in their absence.

Rather, I am talking about personal pride, that comfort zone that is reached with self and which comes from a healthy estimate of who one is as a person. As Cesar

Chavez, the great labor leader and civil rights activist once said as he reminisced on the life of Dr. Martin Luther King, Jr., no one can humiliate the person who feels pride or oppress the people who are not afraid anymore. This sentiment also mirrors a statement made by former First Lady, Eleanor Roosevelt, a person who exuded high self-esteem and who was one of the most eloquent, if not most feisty First Ladies of America. She expressed that no one can make you feel inferior without your consent. This is a pithy statement which should occupy a very prominent area on our refrigerators or notice boards in our kitchens. Indeed, it should be written, figuratively speaking, on the foreheads of our children.

One of the most pleasing things that has happened in recent times is the growing awareness of the importance of those who suffer from various disabilities to continue to contribute to the good of society. This has come about not because of the pity of the "able" among us, but because members of this community have asserted themselves and demonstrated their own significance in building their own lives without the pity or patronage of other people. They celebrate their significance in demanding, not begging, that buildings be built to facilitate their easy mobility from place to place, that they be given good jobs at which they can work at the level of their competence, to participate in competitive sports, and to perform a host of other activities and engagements that others would not think them capable of. Stevie Wonder, the famed song-writer and musician and a man of high self-esteem, continues to amaze and inspire us even though he does not know what a microphone, television set, computer, guitar, piano or any other musical instrument looks like.

My respect for this community of persons was raised recently when I visited a Lowe's improvement store. I needed to do some concrete paving at my house so I bought six bags of quickrete. When I went to have them loaded on to my pickup the young man who attended to me was sitting in a wheel chair. Just as I was about to ask him if someone was coming to put the bags on the truck he moved forward to do it. I stepped forward to assist him and he held out his two hands in protest, so I stood back. With great agility he loaded those bags on to the truck in less than six minutes and wished me well. I was going to offer him a tip, but when I saw his self-confidence I decided against it lest I should shame myself any further.

I had reacted as we all tend to do with people with disability: pity them. In this young man I had come face to face with self-esteem at its best. I felt that I had stepped one notch down from my own self-esteem pedestal. I had felt pity for him but this is not what he wanted. He taught me a lesson from his own inner strength, from the beauty that he perceived within himself, from his intrinsic worth as a person and most importantly, from a celebration of his own significance.

This is what life is about and this is what cultivating a life characterized by a high estimate of ourselves is all about. Having a high estimate of self is more than having a high self-confidence. Confidence comes and goes, but self-esteem as we have sought to define it in this book, is more than just feeling confident about ourselves. It is a state that resides in us, that makes us who we are and helps us to be morally sensitive to the needs of others. I can believe that the heads of the drug cartels or other crime syndicates have high self-confidence in doing the things they do to defy the laws of the land. But, how morally sensitive are they to other people's needs when they trespass on the life and property of others; when they maim and kill with impunity, and when they live in their own misshapen world of iniquity which they equate with happiness? What is significant in this kind of lifestyle as far as the greater good of humanity is concerned?

Ultimate happiness in life is not found until we can come to that place of inner harmony and peace which really are the platforms for our significance. This does not only relate to gaining ownership and control over the pains in our lives but by reaching a level of maturity and healing by which we can now go on to establish good and holistic relations with people and be able to make sound ethical decisions. It also means striving persistently and coura-geously to achieve productive outcomes in our lives by being honest with who we are. Blaming other people and circumstances for who we are or for what we have become are hardly the things that make for honesty or make for significant living.

If we want to achieve significance, then we have to stop running from ourselves and face the awful but liberating truth that we are indeed the problem that need to be fixed. We have got to get a grip of ourselves and begin to deal creatively with the issues that only we alone can solve, with necessary professional help, of course, where neces-sary. But, we have got to take the initiative. No one else can be responsible for the changes we know we have to make in our lives. There may be a lot of blame to go around and perhaps we have been greatly wronged by what others have done to us or said about us. But we must ask ourselves this question: Are we going to spend the rest of our lives stewing over what others have done us, plotting strategies of revenge and shivering in the frigid cold or simmering in the hot waters of hate? Or, are we going to look within ourselves and realize that while we cannot change other people's opinion of us, we can change our opinion of ourselves and begin the long trek along the pathway of healing and holistic living? We may want to close the book at this point, shut our eyes and begin to reflect on these questions.

Part of celebrating our significance is knowing how to regenerate ourselves which involves removing the clutter from our lives. I admit that I am the quintessential pack rat. Like many people I find it difficult to throw away things. Recently, I set myself the task of cleaning up my garage which meant going into some old boxes and throwing out paper and books that I did not even remember I had. At the end of the exercise, the place looked clean, felt fresh and airy and the light returned to dark corners. I congratulated myself for a job well done.

That bit of work made me think that just as how we keep cluttered garages and rooms, so are we inclined to keep a lot of clutter and junk in our lives which weigh us down and cause us not to be as productive as we ought. I believe that if we are going to live happy and abundant lives characterized by high self-esteem we need to identify the things that need to be removed and parked by the curb. What I have realized is that many of the things that we have accumulated we do not need anyway. We make little use of them in our daily lives. Deep down we know that we should have let go of them a long time ago, yet we have held on to them until they have come to occupy a prominent place in our lives. Having achieved a place of legitimacy it is much harder to remove them.

Part of the exercise is to de-clutter our minds of toxic thoughts that have poisoned our relationships with others, that have caused hurt, resentment and bitterness to build up over the years. These things weigh us down, make us unhealthy and leave no room for more productive, healthy and life-giving thoughts to develop and thrive. Deep down we know that if we are to move on successfully we have to summon up the courage to remove them. Self-regeneration is not possible as long as they remain as excess baggage weighing us down.

The power to choose is in our hands and we alone have the power to accept or reject the negatives that life throws at us. Remember that life at its best can be quite brutal and no one is owed a free lunch, no matter what any political philosophy tells us. We have the power of self-regeneration, of rebirth. As a gardener I never cease to marvel at nature's ability to regenerate itself. I once had a mango tree that I thought had been killed in a freeze. There was just a dried, rotting stump left where a once thriving tree stood. I was going to pull it up but suddenly decided against it hoping that it would show life again. When the spring came I saw a beautiful shoot where the stump stood. Today, it is once more a thriving tree that has borne fruit more than a few times. It has been hit by many frosts but not vanquished in its fight to stay alive.

As I look at this natural miracle I am inclined to think that life is pretty much like this. We have to regenerate ourselves. When we come to a place where we are stuck in low self-esteem we can know that this is not the end of the world, but that there is a power within us that cries out to be set free, the power to regenerate and recreate ourselves. It is the power that allows us to bounce back from a setback and to turn quicksand into sandbars. It is the power that helps us to transcend the limitations of time and space and allows us a connection with that deeper, spiritual self that lies deep down inside of us, and which allows us to tap into our inner beauty, the essence of our intrinsic worth as persons. Finally, it is the power to value your life highly and to maintain that value against the tides of doubt, cynicism and pessimism that rise up against it. This is the essence of what high self-esteem is all about.

www.ingramcontent.com/pod-product-compliance
Lightning Source LLC
Chambersburg PA
CBHW071850020426
42331CB00007B/1939

9 780971 304932